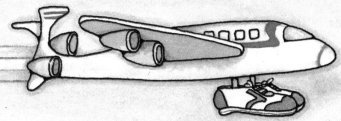

Oh, So Silly!

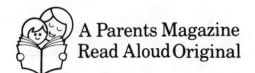

Oh, So Silly!

By Susan Alton Schmeltz
pictures by Maryann Cocca-Leffler

Parents Magazine Press • New York

Text Copyright © 1983 by Susan Alton Schmeltz.
Illustrations Copyright © 1983 by Maryann Cocca-Leffler.
Printed in the United States of America.
10 9 8 7 6 5 4

Library of Congress Cataloging in Publication Data
Schmeltz, Susan Alton.
    Oh, so silly!
    Summary: A child's variety of experiences on a trip
with Grandpa include a plane, a train, the beach,
camping, a country fair—and lots of silly things.
    [1. Vacations—Fiction.   2. Stories in rhyme]
I. Cocca-Leffler, Maryann, 1958-   ill.   II. Title.
PZ8.3.S364Oh   1984   [E]   83-23754
ISBN 0-8193-1122-7

Guess what! I'm going on a trip!
My Grandpa's taking me.
So come along and laugh with us
At silly things we'll see.

Our first stop is the airport. I
Just know I'll like to fly.
Oh, look! There's something silly now.
I see it walking by.

The plane is here and it's quite clear
It's not like most I've seen.
Don't point or stare. But look down there.
Do you see what I mean?

I'm glad we get to climb on board.
We're really on our way!
And soon we'll reach the beach where I
Can run and romp and play.

I love the sea. I love the sand.
I love the salty air.
And just like Grandpa promised, things
Are silly everywhere!

The beach got hot and so we thought
That we would take a swim.
Quick! Tell me! Are things silly here?
Or is the light just dim?

It's time for bed. Lights out. Good night!
Today was really great.
I see a few more silly things.
It must be getting late!

The sun is up and so are we.
We've found a fishing stream.
I think it's even stranger here
Than other spots we've seen!

Tonight we'll eat and sleep outside
Beside this quiet lake.
I wonder. Am I dreaming this?
Or am I wide awake?

Yum! Breakfast in a restaurant.
I hope they'll let us stay
Though we've still got the giggles over
Things from yesterday.

We have a busy time ahead.
Our first stop is the fair.
Are you surprised that silly things
Are happening here and there?

Now Grandpa wants to buy a gift
For me to take back home.
Do you see lots of silly things?
If so, you're not alone!

We're having fun here in the sun,
So won't you join us please?
We've borrowed bikes to ride beside
This grove of silly trees.

A barnyard is the perfect spot
To eat our picnic lunch.
I'll count some sillies while I chew
And chomp and munch and crunch.

It's our last stop. We're heading home,
And though we liked the plane,
My Grandpa thinks it might be fun
To ride back on the train.

This station is a busy place.
They say our train is late.
But I don't mind. Now we can find
More sillies while we wait.

I'll just sit back. The seats are soft.
I know I'll like the view.
Already I am sure I see
A silly thing or two.

We're back at last. Our trip was fun.
I want to go next year!
But now it's nice to be at home...

There's nothing silly here!

About the Author

SUSAN ALTON SCHMELTZ loves to travel. Like the characters in this book, she has seen some very silly things. A few years back, while driving through the state of Washington, she and her husband saw a convertible coming toward them. The riders in front looked normal enough, but the full-grown horse in the back seat definitely seemed out of place!

Ms. Schmeltz also wrote PETS I WOULDN'T PICK for Parents. She lives in Leawood, Kansas.

About the Artist

MARYANN COCCA-LEFFLER especially
enjoyed illustrating this book because she
doesn't get to travel as much as she would
like. "Since the characters seemed to be
having so much fun, I decided to join
them," she says. "I'm on a few pages
starting at the airport, where I'm waiting
on line right next to Grandpa."

In addition to illustrating children's
books, Ms. Cocca-Leffler, with her
husband, founded a greeting card
company featuring her work. She lives in
Saugus, Massachusetts.